oks

late show

The 1920s

John Peacock

Fashion Sourcebooks The 1920s

With 295 illustrations

For Henrietta Webb

© 1997 Thames & Hudson Ltd,
London

Reprinted 2000

British Library Cataloguing-in-
Publication Data
A catalogue record for this book is
available from the British Library

ISBN 0-500-27932-2

Printed and bound in Slovenia
by Mladinska Knjiga

Contents

Introduction   7

The Plates

1920   9

1921   13

1922   17

1923   21

1924   25

1925   29

1926   33

1927   37

1928   41

1929   45

Descriptions   49

Chart of the Development of 1920s Fashion   60
Biographies of Designers   62
Sources for 1920s Fashion   64
Acknowledgments   64

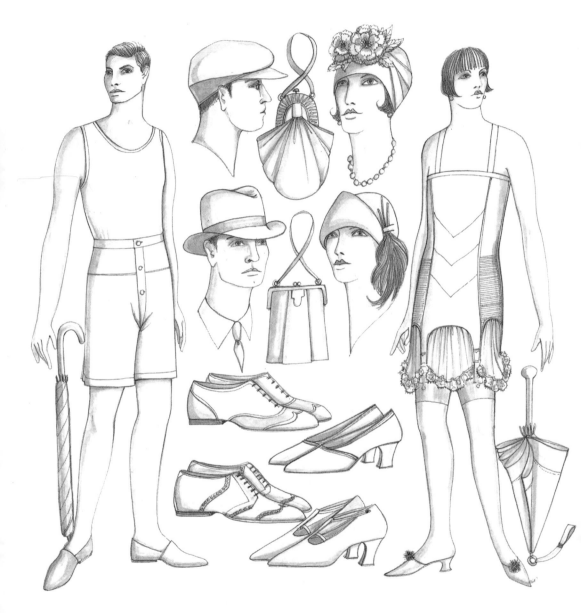

The fashionable woman of the 1920s wanted to look youthful, like an androgynous schoolboy or a pubescent schoolgirl, flat-chested and hipless; at the same time she wanted independence and freedom. These factors forced changes in fashion. Even a casual browse through the pages of this Fashion Sourcebook will reveal just how slowly such changes took place year by year between 1920 and 1929 and just how subtle they were. Yet the result was radical. The corseted woman of the previous decade, with her hobble skirts and huge hats, looks as if she has come from another world when compared to the 'modern' woman of the second half of this decade. The 'designed' proportions of what was considered to be the perfect, fashionable 1920s female body evolved from the elaborately trimmed dress with its high waist position and ankle-length skirt, at the beginning of the period, to the simple, sparsely decorated, shapeless tube with a hip-level 'waistline' and a skirt barely covering the knees, at the decade's end.

At the same time, new fabrics became available, such as kasha, a soft and extremely supple flannel made from a mixture of wool and goat hair; 'art' silk, an easily washed artificial material made from rayon; flamingo, a silk and wool mix with the fashionable crêpe look; satin doubleface, with satin on one side and moiré on the other; and wool, silk and cotton jersey, a fine, machine-knitted fabric previously used only for underwear. Coloured and patterned, this last fabric became a firm favourite of Coco Chanel, and all these innovative materials stimulated thinking about new ways of exploiting their particular qualities and characters. Early use of bias-cutting can clearly be seen in the later pages of this Sourcebook.

As far as men's fashions were concerned, developments in style, colour and cut during the 1920s were painfully slow. In consequence, they require fewer illustrations – the minor differences that do occur in the basic trends have been shown, on average, with one example for each page.

In the main, the fashions I have illustrated are such as would have been worn by the middle or upper-middle classes and by people who, while not being 'dedicated followers of fashion', would have had a keen interest in the latest styles.

The sources from which I have drawn – chiefly from Great Britain, North America and France – include contemporary magazines, journals and catalogues; museum collections; original photographs and my own costume collection.

This Sourcebook is divided into ten sections, each of which includes four subdivisions covering Day Wear, Evening Wear (alternately, on two occasions, Wedding Wear), Sports and Leisure Wear and a section on either Underwear or Accessories. Following the main illustrations are ten pages of schematic drawings accompanied by detailed notes about each example, giving particulars of colour, fabric, cut and trimming as well as other useful information. Then follow two pages of drawings which illustrate the decade 'at a glance' and which demonstrate the evolution of the period and its main development trends.

Biographies of the most important international fashion designers of the decade are also included as well as a list of further reading suggestions into the fashion styles of this fascinating period.

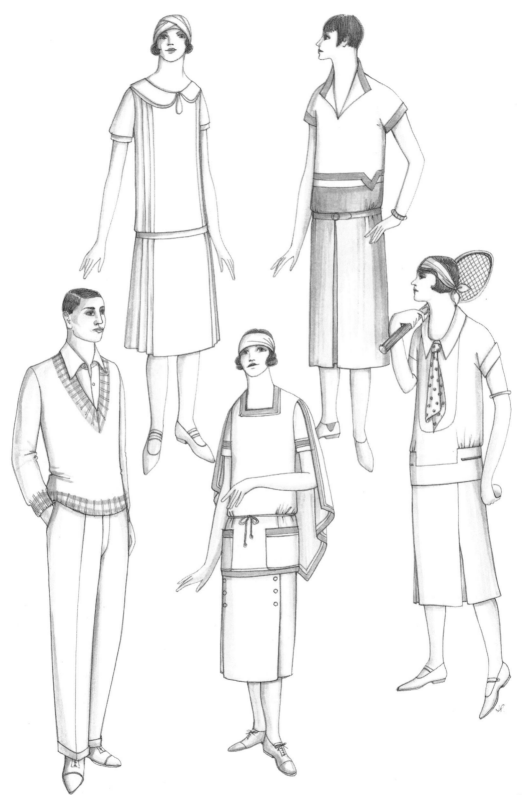

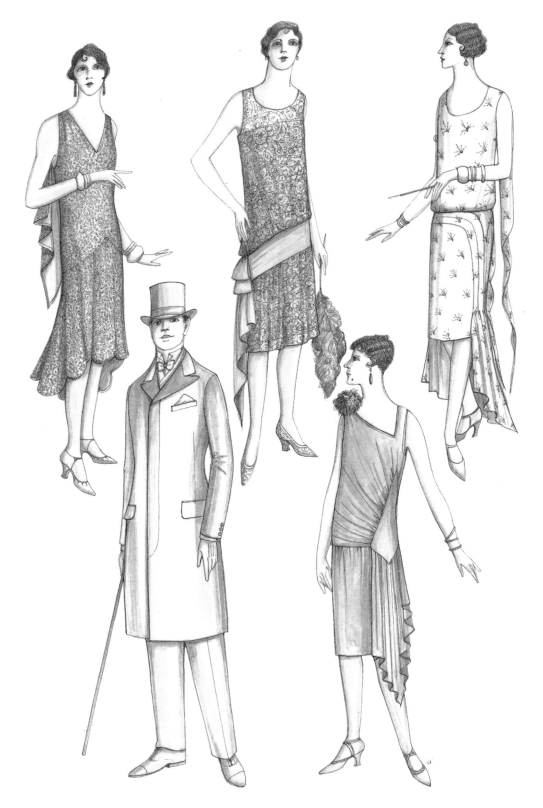

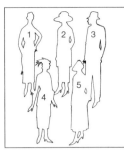
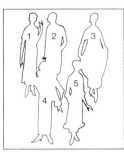

1920 Day Wear

1 Mid-calf-length beige wool dress, high waist marked with brown wool belt, matching binding on scooped neckline, hems of long dolman sleeves, shaped yoke seam, edges of hip-level patch pockets and fringing on floating panels. Silk stockings. Brown leather shoes with buckle trim, pointed toes, louis heels. **2** Pale blue two-piece suit: long edge-to-edge high-waisted jacket, buttoned belt, small collar, wide lapels and front edges bound with light brown silk to match flaps on large patch pockets, button trim from wrist to elbow on tight inset sleeves; narrow mid-calf-length skirt. Hip-length cream silk blouse with low square neckline and sham front-button opening. Hat with large crown and wide brim covered with cream silk, trimmed with brown silk threaded through buckle. Leather button boots with suede uppers, pointed toes, louis heels. **3** Dark blue wool two-piece suit: double-breasted fitted jacket, wide lapels, angled flap pockets, cuffed sleeves; narrow ankle-length trousers with turn-ups. Striped collar-attached shirt. Striped silk tie. Black trilby with wide band. Leather gloves. **4** High-waisted pale green crêpe-de-chine dress, square neckline trimmed with green lace and velvet ribbon to match trim on belt and hems of three-tier skirt, inset sleeves with button trim from wrist to elbow. Green hat with narrow brim, green and cream feather trim. Green leather shoes with cross-over straps, pointed toes, louis heels. **5** Mid-calf-length light brown waterproofed cotton raincoat, fly fastening from under high buckled belt, large collar and wide lapels, vertical welt pockets, inset sleeves with deep armholes, buckle-and-strap trim. Hat with upturned brim, fabric flower trim. Leather shoes with high tongues and buckle trim, pointed toes, louis heels.

Evening Wear

1 Ankle-length violet silk dress with wide scooped neckline, lilac silk-chiffon overdress, high waist marked with wide band of fine silver lace, matching hems of short dolman sleeves and bordering hem of wrapover skirt. Long grey kid gloves. Long bead necklace. Silver leather shoes, rosette trim, pointed toes, louis heels. **2** Double-breasted black wool tailcoat, worn open, small collar, wide silk lapels, matching self-fabric buttons, narrow trousers with no turn-ups. Single-breasted white piqué waistcoat with shawl collar. White shirt with wing collar. White bow-tie. White leather gloves. Black patent-leather pumps, petersham ribbon bow trim. **3** Ankle-length yellow and gold patterned silk-velvet dress, low neckline, high waist position and hemline trimmed with ruched self-fabric; pale yellow silk-chiffon overdress, long dolman sleeves with frilled hems, full skirt with uneven hemline. Gold satin shoes, bow trim, pointed toes, louis heels. **4** Ankle-length double-breasted printed silk-velvet coat, single wrapover fastening, shawl collar faced with satin and trimmed with fox fur which matches cuffs of wide dolman sleeves. Kid gloves. Fine leather shoes trimmed with silver and jet buckles. **5** Ankle-length black crêpe-de-chine dress with narrow shoulder straps; black silk-chiffon overdress, low scooped neckline, high waist position marked with pleated self-fabric belt, trimmed with bunch of silk violets, elbow-length inset sleeves trimmed with curled ostrich feathers to match hem of gathered mid-calf-length skirt. Black satin shoes trimmed with tiny jet buckles, pointed toes, louis heels.

Sports and Leisure Wear

1 Golf. Three-piece brown and cream checked wool suit: fitted single-breasted jacket, flap pockets, single breast pocket, wide lapels; collarless single-breasted waistcoat; knee-length plus-fours. Collar-attached shirt. Wool tweed tie. Brown wool tweed cap. Leather gloves. Long wool socks with turned-down patterned cuffs. Brown leather brogues with fringed tongues. **2** Country wear. Two-piece green and black wool-tweed suit: long single-breasted jacket with pleated side panels, wide lapels, black velvet collar, matching sleeve cuffs, half-belt and self-fabric buttons; ankle-length skirt with pleated side panels. Brown felt hat, large crown with deep band, wide brim turned up at back. Lace-up shoes, pointed toes, stacked heels. **3** Tennis. Long knitted-silk blouse, wide pleated belt, pointed peter-pan collar, shirt sleeves with wide cuffs, single breast patch pocket, fancy stitching to match hems. Mid-calf-length pleated wool skirt. Straw hat with large crown and wide flat brim. Lace-up white canvas shoes. **4** Golf. Three-piece grey wool-tweed suit: long jacket with mock double-breasted fastening, high waist-belt, hip-level pockets, tight inset sleeves with deep cuffs; collarless single-breasted waistcoat; narrow mid-calf-length skirt, hand-stitched edges and detail. Soft wool hat with gathered crown and narrow upturned brim trimmed with braid. Two-tone leather shoes, fringed tongues, pointed toes, flat heels. **5** Sports wear. Hip-length single-breasted wool-tweed jacket, cuffed raglan sleeves, narrow shawl collar, tie-belt and large patch pockets. Straight mid-calf-length beige wool skirt. Collar-attached shirt. Wool-tweed tie. Hat with large crown and wide brim, large bow trim. Leather shoes with bar straps.

Underwear and Negligee

1 Hip-length embroidered pink cotton-satin corset, light boning and top-stitching, front hook-and-bar fastening, back lacing, lace and ribbon trimming, four elasticated suspenders. Fine white cotton chemise with scalloped edges and openwork embroidery, double ribbon shoulder straps. Pale blue velvet house slippers, pointed toes, louis heels. **2** Fine cotton combination chemise and drawers, front opening top to high waist position, fastening with self-fabric buttons, pintuck and lace decoration, double ribbon shoulder straps, drawers gathered from high waist position to knee-level forming frill, pintuck and lace trim. Velvet house shoes trimmed with silk pom-pons. **3** Fine cotton knee-length red wool dressing gown, wide quilted red silk shawl collar with corded edge matching deep cuffs of inset sleeves and cuffs of large hip-level patch pockets, cord tie-belt with tasselled ends. Red and grey striped cotton pyjamas. Red leather step-in house slippers. **4** Blue silk nightdress, low square neckline edged with cream lace and coffee-coloured silk ribbon to match hems of wide cap sleeves and inset band above hemline, high waist marked with ribbon belt. Pale blue satin house slippers with rosette trim. **5** Wrapover ankle-length peach-coloured satin dressing gown, deep shawl collar with self-frilled edge and trimmed with re-embroidered lace border which matches deep cuffs of inset sleeves and large hip-level patch pockets, high waist position marked with self-fabric tie-belt with tasselled ends. Embroidered satin mules, pointed toes, low heels.

1921 Day Wear

1 Single-breasted mid-calf-length fur coat, fastening with three outsized buttons, large collar over elbow-length cape, inset sleeves with deep cuffs, concealed pockets. Straw hat with wide brim and large crown, satin band and bow trim. Leather shoes, flower rosette trim, pointed toes, louis heels. **2** Double-breasted checked wool-tweed overcoat, inset buttoned belt, wide lapels, narrow inset sleeves, hip-level patch-and-flap pockets, top-stitched edges and detail. Narrow trousers with turn-ups. Brown felt trilby with high crown, brim turned up at back and sides. Leather gloves. Leather lace-up shoes, pointed toecaps. **3** Mid-calf-length double-breasted dark red linen coat, fastening with two outsized plastic buttons which match trim on flared cuffs of inset sleeves; pleated side skirt panel matches sleeve cuffs; side bodice above low waistline trimmed with narrow braid to match sleeves; narrow roll collar. Fox-fur stole. Dark red velvet hat, feather trim. Leather gloves. Leather shoes. **4** Two-piece cream linen suit: hip-length single-breasted jacket, fastening with large buttons which match trim on hem of narrow inset sleeves and on decorative side panel seams above hemline, shaped shawl collar; mid-calf-length straight skirt. Collarless single-breasted striped linen waistcoat. Brown straw hat, large brim swept up on one side, ribbon trim. Long-handled parasol. Brown leather shoes trimmed with round buckles. **5** Pale blue silk dress, low round neckline, mid-calf-length gathered skirt, shorter overdress in self-fabric with open front, strap-and-button fastening, draped self-fabric belt, narrow inset sleeves trimmed at wrist with dark blue lace to match small collar, hem of overskirt and bodice of underdress. Dark blue straw hat trimmed with small plums. Long-handled parasol. Shoes with wide bar strap.

Evening Wear

1 Ankle-length sleeveless yellow silk dress, wide neckline, deep cape collar, embroidered edge repeated on hemline of gathered skirt and tiered side panels, unfitted hip-length bodice, draped self-fabric belt decorated with bunch of silk primroses. Yellow satin shoes trimmed with small round buckles, pointed toes, louis heels. **2** Asymmetric green lace bodice with low V-shaped neckline, asymmetric ankle-length green crêpe-de-chine dress draped from shoulder to opposite hip, jewelled clip, waterfall of self-fabric and green lace to below hemline of straight skirt. Silver kid shoes trimmed with jewelled buckles. **3** Ankle-length grey crêpe-de-chine dress, unfitted hip-length bodice, straight skirt, wide neckline trimmed with grey lace border to match motifs above hemline of mid-calf-length gathered silk-chiffon overskirt, elbow-length inset sleeves with double row of padded and gathered binding which matches three rows on overskirt. Silver kid shoes, large tongues trimmed with tiny silver buckles. **4** Unfitted ankle-length black silk-georgette overdress, wide shaped neckline and head of sleeves embroidered with black glass beads to match border of curved hemline up to hip-level of open sides, low waistline marked by black sequined belt from side to back which matches cuffs of gathered sleeves; black silk-crêpe underdress. Black silk shoes. **5** Hip-length dark red watered-silk cape with high ruched buttoned collar, elbow-length shaped yoke, uneven hemline trimmed with frilled black lace. Ankle-length black silk dress; black lace overdress with scalloped hemline. Black silk shoes trimmed with ribbon flowers, pointed toes, louis heels.

Sports and Leisure Wear

1 Tennis. Hip-length cream cotton top, scooped neckline, collar top-stitched in dark blue to match cuffs of three-quarter-length inset sleeves, front panel seams and shaped hemline, embroidered motif on bodice between collar points, blue stiffened silk belt threaded through panel seams, matching self-fabric buttons. Ankle-length box-pleated cream wool skirt. Natural straw hat, large crown with flat top and striped band, wide flat brim. Cream cotton stockings. Cream canvas lace-up shoes. **2** Golf. Hip-length dark green knitted-wool top, pointed collar, strap opening, long inset sleeves with shaped stitched cuffs matching stitched hemline. Ankle-length green tweed skirt, button opening from waist to hem, knife-pleated panels from side front. Dark brown felt hat with large crown, petersham ribbon band, wide flat brim. Brown leather boots laced to mid-calf, pointed toecaps. **3** Riding. Single-breasted mid-thigh-length brown wool coat with flared skirts, inset buttoned belt, wide lapels, tight inset sleeves with stitched cuffs, four patch pockets with buttoned flaps. Beige riding breeches, laced on side seam. Felt hat, large flared crown, petersham band, wide flat brim. Leather gloves. Short lace-up leather boots. Knee-high leather gaiters, strap-and-buckle fastening. **4** Bathing. Two-piece navy and white striped knitted-cotton bathing costume, hip-length top, low square neckline, plain navy collar which matches cuffs of short inset sleeves, buttoned belt, central bodice panel, self-fabric buttons and cuffs of knee-length drawers. Spotted cotton headscarf. Rubber bathing shoes with crossed straps to mid-calf. **5** Bathing. Two-piece sleeveless blue and white striped knitted-cotton bathing costume, hip-length top, low round neckline and armholes bound in plain white cotton to match hems of top and drawers, buttoned opening on shoulder.

Accessories

1 Leather shoes, turned-down tongues with perforated decoration and fringed ends. **2** White kid shoes, button trim, blue heels and toecaps. **3** Straw hat, large crown trimmed with silk, narrow brim trimmed with silk flowers. **4** Fine straw hat, large crown draped with silk, wide brim trimmed with silk violets. **5** Leather shoes, perforated decoration and top-stitching. **6** Two-tone lace-up leather shoes. **7** Dusty-pink crocheted two-piece: hip-length top, large collar with fancy stitching which matches hems of top and inset sleeves, threaded hip-level belt; pleated skirt. **8** Orange scarf with inset bands of dark green, matching fringe. Straw hat with wide upturned brim edged with dark green ribbon, trimmed with silk flowers. **9** Green silk bag, metal frame and fastening, ribbon handle. **10** Shoes, wide bar straps, perforated decoration, matching pointed toes. **11** Black crêpe bag, metal frame and clasp. **12** Brown wool peaked cap. **13** Grey homburg with black petersham band. **14** Two-tone leather bag, personal initials, metal frame and fastening, rouleau handle. **15** Leather bag with flap front, stud fastening, long strap. **16** Lace-up leather shoes with front seamed panel, no toecaps. **17** Tan leather brogues, perforated decoration, shaped toecaps. **18** Leather sandals, T-strap-and-buckle fastening, no toecaps. **19** Black leather shoes, high tongues trimmed with petersham bows. **20** Cream suede shoes, cut-out pattern, strap-and-button fastening. **21** Hat with tall crown, trimmed ribbon band and loops, bound brim. **22** Two-tone brogues in brown and white leather. **23** Straw hat, large crown and wide brim draped with black lace. **24** Lace-up leather brogues, fringed tongues, stacked heels. **25** Cream satin T-strap shoes with open sides. **26** Straw hat, large crown, small brim, chiffon and silk flower trim.

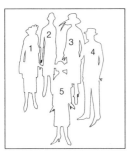  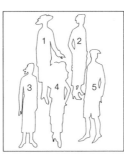 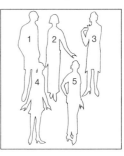

1922 Day Wear

1 Two-piece grey wool suit: long unfitted single-breasted jacket, long narrow collar, wide lapels, single-button fastening at low waist-level, flared skirt with gathered side panels and single box pleats from hip-level side belts, flared sleeves; mid-calf-length skirt with box pleats. Grey silk blouse. Grey fox-fur stole and matching muff. Felt hat with upturned brim, crown decorated with large pink silk roses. Grey leather shoes, buckle trim, pointed toes. **2** Brown and pink striped silk dress, hip-length unfitted bodice, waist marked with chain-belt, round neckline, shaped yoke, three-quarter-length sleeves, mid-calf-length skirt gathered from hipline, decorative use of stripes. Shoes with pointed toes. **3** Blue and cream checked wool dress, hip-level unfitted bodice, V-shaped neckline, three-quarter-length inset sleeves, half yoke, inset band of bias-cut fabric at hip-level, bound pockets and button trim, mid-calf-length gathered skirt. Blue and cream embroidered blouse with full sleeves. Large hat with gathered crown, wide brim trimmed with two feathers. Leather shoes, wide buttoned ankle straps. **4** Two-piece blue-grey wool suit: fitted double-breasted jacket, narrow lapels, patch pockets, button trim; narrow ankle-length trousers with turn-ups. Shirt with buttoned collar. Checked silk tie. Straw boater, dark ribbon band. Blue and white leather shoes, pointed toes. **5** Mid-calf-length single-breasted unfitted fawn wool coat, wide lapels, large cape collar trimmed with brown ribbon-embroidered braid which matches hems of flared sleeves, band at hip-level and large self-fabric buttons. Large brown silk hat, high crown trimmed with wide ribbon band, loops and bows. Leather gloves. Dark flesh-coloured silk stockings. Leather shoes, stitched detail, pointed toes, louis heels.

Evening Wear

1 Mid-calf-length bright pink crêpe-de-chine evening dress, unfitted bodice, wide scooped neckline, short dolman sleeves, low waistline marked with wide black silk-taffeta cummerbund decorated on one side with outsized bow and waterfall with bead-fringed edge; black embroidered-net gathered overskirt with scalloped hem. Black silk shoes, wide ankle straps, buckle trim. **2** Mid-calf-length dark pink crêpe-de-chine dinner dress, unfitted bodice, gathered skirt, underpart of flared sleeves embroidered with bright pink and dark blue glass beads matching neckline and hem of underskirt, deep hipband decorated with self-fabric roses, coat-effect overbodice, upper sleeves and long side panels in plain dark blue crêpe-de-chine. **3** Two-piece black wool suit: single-breasted fitted jacket, wide silk lapels, hip-level piped pockets, breast pocket with silk handkerchief, narrow sleeves with sewn cuffs; narrow trousers, no turn-ups. White cotton starched shirt, wing collar. Black silk bow-tie. Black patent-leather pumps, petersham bow trim. **4** Yellow silk dance frock, hip-length unfitted bodice, low waist marked with black velvet ribbon belt to match edges of scalloped collar, cuffs of short sleeves and gathered tiered skirt. Black satin shoes with double bar straps. **5** Black silk-velvet evening dress, hip-length unfitted bodice, straight ankle-length wrapover skirt, low waist marked with pleated black chiffon belt, large beaded jet motif on side hip which matches clasps on each side of wide neckline and tasselled hem of open waterfall chiffon sleeves. Black silk shoes, pointed toes, louis heels.

Sports and Leisure Wear

1 Country wear. Single-breasted hip-length rust-coloured wool jacket, fastening with two large self-fabric buttons, collar, revers and edges top-stitched to match cuffs of raglan sleeves, stitched cuffs of patch pockets and threaded low-placed belt. Mid-calf-length rust, cream and green checked wool-tweed skirt. Straw boater trimmed with decorative ribbon. Shoes with buckle trim, pointed toes. **2** Sports wear. Long single-breasted beige knitted-wool jacket, fastening with single horn button which matches trim on shaped shawl collar and flaps on patch pockets, inset sleeves with deep cuffs, fringed hem. Mid-calf-length camel-coloured wool skirt, buttoned side vents to knee-level, deep waistband. Striped cotton shirt, plain collar. Knotted silk scarf. Dark red beret with long brown tassel. Leather shoes. **3** Tennis. Fine white cotton blouse, low fastening with two self-fabric buttons which match deep cuffs on raglan sleeves, long shaped roll collar. Mid-calf-length linen skirt, top-stitched front panel with button opening to knee-level, hip-level welt pockets. Hair tied back with scarf. Canvas sports shoes. **4** Holiday wear. Fine white cotton-voile dress, hip-length unfitted bodice gathered into hipband with threaded ribbon belt which matches detail under square neckline, lace collar matching cuffs on three-quarter-length sleeves, mid-calf-length tiered skirt. Hat trimmed with artificial fruit and silk ribbon. Parasol. Leather shoes, buckle trim, pointed toes. **5** Golf. Two-piece light brown wool suit: single-breasted jacket with buttoned belt, narrow sleeves, stitched cuffs, welt pockets; knee-length breeches. Collar-attached shirt. Tweed tie. Checked wool peaked cap. Leather gloves. Knee-length knitted-wool socks. Leather boots. Long buttoned gaiters.

Underwear and Negligee

1 Fine cream wool combination top and drawers, shallow top-stitched stand collar matching button-through strap opening and cuffs of inset shirt sleeves, fly opening from base of strap to crotch. **2** Sleeveless ankle-length peach-coloured crêpe-de-chine nightdress, low scooped neckline edged with narrow lace, shaped yoke decorated with appliqué embroidery, tiny pintucks over bustline, low-placed self-fabric tie-belt. Boudoir cap in matching fabric, turned back brim with fine lace edging, self-fabric flower applied to each corner. Embroidered velvet slippers with scalloped edges, pointed toes. **3** Pale blue satin petticoat, low scooped neckline infilled with pale coffee-coloured lace matching wide shoulder straps and uneven hemline, gathered side panels from hip-level. Blue velvet house shoes, pointed toes, high louis heels. **4** Pink rubber bust flattener with narrow adjustable shoulder straps, flaps button to top-stitched girdle reaching from waist to hip, side-laced opening from hem to high hip-level, four elasticated and adjustable suspenders. Flesh-coloured silk stockings. Velvet house shoes, pointed toes, louis heels. **5** Two-piece pale green silk pyjama suit, hip-length top, short dolman sleeves trimmed with pale cream lace to match low round neckline, central motif and hems of top and ankle-length straight-cut trousers. Green velvet mules trimmed with cream satin, pointed toes, low louis heels.

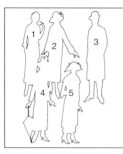

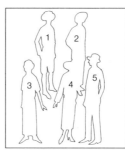

1923 Day Wear

1 Ankle-length grey velvet dress, unfitted bodice to low waistline, open jacket-effect overbodice with long shawl collar, underbodice forming square neckline, smock trim matching line above narrow cuffs of three-quarter-length inset flared sleeves, skirt gathered from hipline, low waistline marked with black velvet sash and outsized black plastic buckle. Black leather shoes, buckle trim.
2 Mid-calf-length grey wool coat, double-breasted wrapover front, fastening with three large carved buttons which match trim on outsized collar, inset sleeves, deep cuffs. Large black varnished straw hat, high crown draped with black chiffon, narrow turned-down brim trimmed with a spray of feathers. Leather shoes with buckle and looped trim, high heels. **3** Knee-length double-breasted dark blue wool overcoat, wide lapels, flap pockets, stitched sleeve cuffs. Narrow ankle-length trousers with turn-ups. Shirt worn with stiff collar and collar pins. Striped silk tie. Black bowler hat. Leather gloves. Lace-up leather shoes, pointed toecaps. Walking stick.
4 Ankle-length sage green wool coat, wrapover front held in place by buckled belt, wide combination collar and revers decorated with fine silk braid which matches side panels of bodice and skirts, long raglan sleeves, half-cuffs fastened with self-fabric buttons. Brimless silk and velvet hat trimmed with silk and velvet ribbon loops and bows. Long-handled umbrella. Leather bar-strap shoes. **5** Ankle-length pale turquoise afternoon dress, low waist marked with two buttoned lace belts which match edging on deep collar, elbow-length flared sleeves, hem of overskirt and underbodice. Straw hat with upswept brim, large crown trimmed with grey, pink and turquoise silk flowers. Bar-strap shoes.

Wedding Wear

1 Ice blue silk-crêpe dress, unfitted bodice gathered into low waist position, wide belt embroidered with self-coloured glass beads matching trim on wide square neckline, at elbow-level on wide flared cuffs of tight inset sleeves and on scalloped hemline of gathered skirt, mid-calf-length at front forming short train at back. Tiara of wax flowers and leaves, long silk-tulle veil. Satin shoes with cross-over straps, pointed toes. **2** Single-breasted black wool tailcoat fastening with single button, wide lapels. Single-breasted collarless grey wool waistcoat. Grey wool trousers. White shirt, wing collar. Grey tie. Black top hat. Black shoes with buttoned spats.
3 Pale pink silk-taffeta dress, unfitted bodice to low waist, wide scooped neckline with self-fabric ruched detail matching large rosettes on mid-calf-length gathered overskirt, short inset sleeves, ankle-length self-fabric underskirt. Tiara of silk and wax flowers, matching posy on one shoulder and centres of rosettes on skirt, long silk-tulle veil. Long white kid gloves. White kid shoes with wide bar straps, pointed toes, louis heels. **4** Ankle-length cream silk dress, wide neckline with satin insert detail matching three-quarter-length wrapover sleeves, overskirt, bias-cut floating panel and decoration on unfitted bodice; low waist marked with narrow belt. Large straw hat trimmed with silk flowers. Elbow-length gloves. Kid shoes with buckle trim, pointed toes, louis heels.
5 Ankle-length cream silk dress, wide neckline edged with gathered lace frill to match elbow-length sleeves, unfitted bodice to low waist marked with wide self-fabric sash, gathered skirt decorated with horseshoes of flowers, scalloped hem. Cream silk-organdie cloche hat trimmed with flowers. Cream kid shoes.

Sports and Leisure Wear

1 Bicycling. Two-piece grey wool suit: double-breasted hip-length jacket, low-placed buttoned belt, inset sleeves with stitched cuffs, four pleated patch pockets with buttoned flaps; knee breeches, buttoned straps at knee-level. Collar-attached shirt. Felt hat, large crown, upturned brim. Long knitted-wool socks with patterned cuffs. Lace-up leather shoes. **2** Golf. Two-piece green wool-tweed suit: long edge-to-edge collarless jacket, low waist marked with buckled tailored belt, sloping welt pockets, narrow shoulder yoke, inset sleeves; ankle-length skirt with inverted box pleats. Long single-breasted collarless red wool waistcoat. Cream silk blouse, large collar, deep cuffs. Two-tone leather shoes. **3** Tennis. Ankle-length dress, unfitted hip-length white linen bodice, scooped neckline, inset elbow-length sleeves, low waist marked with self-fabric sash, gathered shaping from half yoke, flared blue linen skirt. Natural straw cloche hat trimmed with wide white ribbon band and bow. White canvas sports shoes. **4** Holiday wear. Mid-calf-length pale peach cotton-voile dress, unfitted bodice decorated with self-coloured embroidery above low waistline to match hems of flared inset sleeves, scooped neckline with narrow collar, buckled belt. Natural straw hat, tall crown, wide brim turned back and trimmed with silk flower. Leather shoes, pointed toes, louis heels.
5 Holiday wear. Single-breasted gold, blue and cream striped linen jacket with wide lapels and patch pockets. Collarless single-breasted waistcoat with welt pockets. Narrow ankle-length trousers with turn-ups. Collar-attached shirt. Spotted silk tie. Straw boater with striped band and bow. Two-tone navy and white leather lace-up shoes, pointed toes.

Accessories

1 Silver chainmail bag, engraved frame, clasp fastening, long chain handle, silver bead trim.
2 Beige leather shoes with suede lace-effect trim, pointed toes, louis heels. **3** Dark green leather shoes with perforated decoration.
4 Pale green silk bag, self-fabric-covered metal frame, clasp fastening, long self-fabric rouleau handle. **5** Silver chainmail bag, engraved frame, clasp fastening, plaited handle, tassel trim.
6 Grey felt hat, upturned brim edged and trimmed with pleated petersham braid. Grey fox-fur stole. **7** Hat with tall silk-organdie crown trimmed with wide silk ribbon, wired lace brim.
8 Ruched purple velvet hat with padded brim, self-coloured satin ribbon trim. **9** Top-stitched yellow straw hat, upturned brim, large crown trimmed with silk flowers at back. **10** Felt hat with unstructured outsized brim, trimmed with silk roses.
11 Lace-up tan leather shoes with perforated decoration.
12 Light brown felt trilby, tall crown trimmed with wide dark brown band and bow, curled brim. Collar-attached shirt. Striped tie.
13 Black bowler with curled brim.
14 Cream kid leather shoes, cross-over buttoned straps, pointed toes, louis heels. **15** Navy blue and white lace-up shoes, perforated decoration, pointed toes. **16** Navy blue and white kid shoes with buttoned bar straps, pointed toes, louis heels. **17** Cream lace-up leather shoes with dark green decorative inserts. **18** Black satin shoes with buttoned bar straps, pointed toes, red louis heels. **19** Black leather shoes with wide buttoned ankle straps, pointed toes, louis heels.

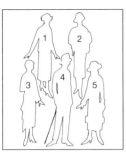

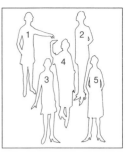

1924 Day Wear

1 Mid-calf-length cream linen dress, unfitted bodice and straight skirt, scooped neckline, brown linen collar matching cuffs of long inset sleeves and inserted front panel, self-fabric buttons from neck to hip-level, low waist marked with narrow buckled tailored belt. Natural straw cloche hat trimmed with wax fruit. Brown leather shoes with wide bar straps. **2** Three-piece natural linen suit: edge-to-edge jacket fastened with self-fabric belt and clasp on low waistline, draped scarf collar, tasselled trim, collar embroidered with pale green silk thread to match hems of flared inset sleeves; mid-calf-length straight skirt. Blouse with straight neckline. Long fur stole. Green felt hat, upturned brim trimmed with feathers. Leather shoes. **3** Hip-length dark blue velvet jacket, double-breasted wrapover front, loop and waterfall side decoration threaded through self-colour beaded braid clasp, matching trim on large collar and hems of inset flared sleeves. Straight mid-calf-length skirt. Black straw cloche hat draped with black silk-chiffon, trimmed with pleated petersham ribbon rosette. Leather gloves. Leather shoes. **4** Single-breasted light brown wool-tweed jacket, narrow lapels, flap pockets. Narrow ankle-length brown flannel trousers with turn-ups. Collar-attached shirt. Wool tie. Fawn felt trilby, trimmed with brown petersham band. Lace-up brown leather shoes. Walking stick. **5** Knee-length burnt-orange velvet coat, unfitted bodice fastened on shoulder and on wide hipband with large decorative buttons, red fox-fur collar matching cuffs of long inset sleeves, hemline, large muff and trim on brim of large dark brown felt hat. Dark brown mid-calf-length dress. Brown leather shoes, pointed toes, high louis heels.

Evening Wear

1 Mid-calf-length black chiffon dress with unfitted bodice and straight skirt cut in one piece, embroidered all over with black glass and crystal beads in leaf patterns, low V-shaped neckline edged with rows of black glass beads to match covered panel seams which extend to below hemline, open plain black chiffon sleeves. Black shoes with wide bar straps. **2** Pale cream crêpe-de-chine dress, straight hip-length unfitted bodice, straight neckline with bust-level beige lace collar falling to hip-level at back, scalloped hemline matching mid-calf-length overskirt, plain crêpe-de-chine loops and waterfalls on side hips. Outsized ostrich-feather fan. Cream silk shoes with tiny rosette trim, pointed toes. **3** Pale pink silk-crêpe sleeveless dress, low scooped neckline, straight unfitted bodice embroidered with beads from side hips and curving up to centre-front to below bust-level, flared and slightly gathered skirt. Satin shoes with double bar straps, pointed toes, high louis heels. **4** Ankle-length pink, red and orange patterned silk-velvet sleeveless dinner dress, wide boat-shaped neckline, asymmetric gold silk overbodice falling in folds from clasp on one shoulder to hipline, floating bias-cut back panel trimmed with feathers to match banded hip and hem detail of open-sided skirt. Feather fan. Fine kid shoes, wide buttoned bar straps with perforated decoration. **5** Lilac silk evening dress, wide boat-shaped neckline, shaped yoke with embroidered and beaded decoration matching bias-cut waterfall sleeves and scalloped hip yoke, bodice gathered into low waistline, gathered bias-cut skirt with handkerchief points and beaded edge. Silk shoes with buckle trim, pointed toes.

Sports and Leisure Wear

1 Holiday wear. Mid-calf-length yellow and blue checked cotton dress, unfitted bodice and straight skirt cut in one piece, square neckline bound with plain blue cotton matching uneven hem of three-quarter-length inset sleeves, side front opening and self-fabric buttons in sets of four, pleated voile trim on opening from neck to waist and repeated on hem of sleeves. Yellow straw cloche hat with white voile trim. Leather shoes with cross-over bar straps. **2** Golf. Double-breasted broad grey and green striped cotton blouse fastening with single self-fabric button, wide revers, narrow yoke, inset shirt sleeves. Straight green tweed skirt, buttoned hipband, hip-level pockets, mock double-breasted button fastening above hemline. Unstructured cotton-velvet hat, sectioned crown, wide brim. Leather shoes with bar straps, low heels. **3** Tennis. Cream double-breasted long collarless tunic, fastening on one side with three self-fabric buttons, boat-shaped neckline, wide binding to above hemline, inset three-quarter-length sleeves, buttoned cuffs, tailored belt. Mid-calf-length cream pleated skirt. Natural straw cloche hat, wide ribbon band. **4** Riding. Single-breasted tan cotton-cord jacket, buttoned belt, box pleats each side front from shaped yoke to hem, large patch pockets with flaps. Light brown knee-breeches. Collar-attached shirt. Wool tie. Long leather boots, laced to knee, strap-and-buckle fastening. **5** Country wear. Mid-calf-length dusty-pink lightweight cotton coat-dress, wrapover front with single-button fastening, long inset sleeves, pink and blue patterned shawl collar matching narrow threaded belt and flared skirt from hip-level. Straw hat, wide brim trimmed with flowers. Leather shoes, cross-over straps, pointed toes.

Underwear and Negligee

1 Fitted flesh-coloured cotton bust flattener, top-stitching, elasticated gusset over side hips, wide shoulder straps, back opening. Flesh-coloured cotton and rubber girdle, elasticated side panels, hook-and-bar front opening, laced adjustment, four adjustable suspenders. Silk stockings. Velvet mules trimmed with satin ribbon bows, louis heels. **2** Two-piece peach silk pyjamas, single-breasted hip-length jacket, loop-and-button fastening, edges embroidered with blanket stitch to match large collar, cuffs of inset sleeves, hip-level welt pockets and turn-ups of ankle-length trousers. Velvet mules trimmed with silk pom-pons. **3** Cotton bust flattener, stitched inserts, adjustable shoulder straps. Cotton girdle, stitched shaped front panel, light boning, four adjustable suspenders. Flesh-coloured silk stockings. House shoes, pointed toes, louis heels. **4** Single-breasted mid-calf-length pale blue and pink crêpe-de-chine housecoat, press-stud fastening concealed under rouleau flower at base of V-shaped neckline, plain pink crêpe-de-chine collar matching cuffs of batwing sleeves and threaded tie-belt with rouleau flower trim. Satin house shoes, pointed toes, louis heels. **5** White cotton petticoat, trimmed on bustline with embroidered and satin ribbon insertions to match hemline, wide shoulder straps and hip-level detail. Velvet mules, pointed toes, louis heels.

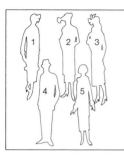

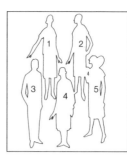

1925 Day Wear

1 Two-piece pale grey wool suit: long jacket, wrapover front fastening with two large self-fabric buttons, wide lapels, large pintucked collar edged with fur to match cuffs of long inset sleeves and hip-length side panels; straight skirt to below knee. Grey felt cloche hat trimmed with pale blue silk ribbon threaded through large buckle. Brown leather shoes, buckle trim. **2** Two-tone navy and cream linen dress, wide boat-shaped neckline, top-stitched edge, self-fabric strap and self-fabric button trim, inset sleeves, flared cuffs, top-stitched detail, unfitted bodice and overskirt effect trimmed with contrasting colour and edged with braid, matching straight skirt. Felt hat, wide upturned brim trimmed with feather pom-pon. Leather shoes, large round buckle trim. **3** Brown wool tweed double-breasted coat, concealed fastening under long roll collar to hip-level buckle trim, waterfall to hem, narrow inset sleeves, fur trim, matching collar. Beige felt cloche hat trimmed with silk ribbon. Beige leather gloves. Leather shoes with bar straps. **4** Double-breasted navy-blue wool jacket, wide lapels, flap pockets, silk handkerchief in breast pocket. Narrow ankle-length grey flannel trousers with turn-ups. Collar-attached shirt. Bow-tie. Pale grey felt trilby. Two-tone lace-up shoes. **5** Hip-length single-breasted dark green leather jacket, fastening with two large plastic buttons, wide lapels and combination collar, top-stitched trim matching cuffs of inset sleeves, buckled belt cut as part of pockets. Leather flower worn on lapel. Checked wool skirt to below knee. Collar-attached shirt. Striped tie. Brimless leather hat, top-stitched trim. Two-tone lace-up leather shoes.

Evening Wear

1 Asymmetric ankle-length gold silk-satin sleeveless overdress, draped from one shoulder to opposite side hip, fixed by bead clasp, open sides, waterfall to hem, sleeveless gold lace underdress, straight neckline, floating panels, scalloped edges to below bustline at front and to hip-level at back. Ostrich-feather fan. Gold kid shoes, pointed toes, high louis heels. **2** Mint green silk-georgette dress embroidered all over with transparent glass beads, sleeveless draped wrapover bodice to hip-level forming low V-shaped neckline, infilled with flesh-coloured silk, narrow hip-level scalloped peplum matching hem of straight skirt. Tiara worn low on forehead. Satin shoes with wide bar straps, pointed toes, louis heels. **3** White silk-net dress embroidered all over with silver glass beads and sequins, straight neckline, narrow beaded shoulder straps, unfitted bodice slightly bloused on hipline, feather flower with jewelled centre on side hip, chiffon waterfall to below knee. Silver kid shoes, pointed toes, louis heels. **4** Mid-calf-length pink silk-taffeta dance dress, sleeveless unfitted bodice, wide V-shaped neckline outlined with rows of lace ribbon, skirt gathered under narrow belt, bow trim and long tails, upturned peplum with lace edge, matching hemline, side panniers formed with garlands of self-fabric roses. Pink silk shoes. **5** Mid-calf-length lilac silk-chiffon dance dress, fitted bodice with horizontal ruching, straight neckline, wide shoulder straps covered with rows of beaded motifs which match ostrich-feather-trimmed hemline of full gathered skirt. Silver kid shoes, pointed toes, louis heels.

Sports and Leisure Wear

1 Tennis. White cotton dress, unfitted bodice with two vertical pleats running from each shoulder under hip-level belt to hem of flared skirt, wide neckline, double peter-pan collar, keyhole opening, short sleeves with narrow cuffs. Draped white cotton turban. White canvas shoes, double bar straps, pointed toes, low heels. **2** Tennis. Unfitted white linen bodice, V-shaped neckline, collar edge trimmed with blue linen to match cuffs of short dolman sleeves, hem of bodice and inset band at waist-level; hip-level tailored belt, flared skirt with centre-front inverted box pleat. Elastic-sided canvas shoes, pointed toes, low heels. **3** Tennis. White knitted-cotton sweater, low V-shaped neckline edged with bands of yellow to match hem and cuffs of inset sleeves. Narrow ankle-length white flannel trousers with turn-ups. White collar-attached shirt, worn open. White canvas lace-up shoes, pointed toecaps. **4** Tennis. Crocheted white cotton top, square neckline edged in blue and yellow to match short inset sleeves, hip-level patch pockets, hemline and edge of inset cape; fine rouleau belt on low waistline. White linen skirt, large box pleat, button trim. White headband. Leather lace-up shoes. **5** Tennis. Hip-length white cotton top, low round neckline, pointed collar, sham shirt front, short cuffed dolman sleeves, piped pockets set into shaped hip yoke. Knotted spotted silk scarf. White linen skirt to below knee, slightly flared, box and inverted box pleats. Wide headband. White canvas shoes with buttoned bar straps, pointed toes, low heels.

Accessories

1 Felt cloche hat, narrow brim, close crown trimmed with silk ribbons. **2** Black leather shoes trimmed with red, red leather heels. **3** Leather shoes with buttoned triple bar straps. **4** Felt cloche hat, notched up-turned brim, petersham ribbon trim, chiffon veil. **5** Black satin shoes, fine cross-over buttoned straps, open sides. **6** Buttoned T-strap shoes, pointed toes, louis heels. **7** Fitted velvet cap with ruched crown, small plain silk peak and narrow brim turned up at back, silk flower trim. **8** Brimless silk cloche, embroidered ribbon and flower motif matching fringed scarf. **9** Ruched velvet evening bag, embroidered central panel, clasp fastening, long ribbon handle. **10** Brimless cloche hat trimmed with petersham ribbon and silk roses. **11** Brimless cloche hat draped and trimmed with silk-organdie bow. **12** Small fan-shaped leather bag, initialled inset panel, metal frame, clasp fastening, long handle. **13** Top-stitched green felt cloche hat, small front brim, crown trimmed with silk butterfly. **14** Linen straw sunhat, domed crown, wide band, narrow brim. **15** Pink crêpe bag made from pleated leaf-shaped pieces, metal frame, clasp fastening, ribbon handle. **16** Silver satin evening bag, silver frame, clasp fastening, long rouleau handle. **17** Small brocade evening bag, flap with stud fastening, self-fabric metal handle. **18** Two-tone lace-up leather shoes. **19** Embroidered velvet evening bag, silver frame, clasp fastening, ribbon handle. **20** Grey felt trilby, tall crown, black ribbon band, wide brim.

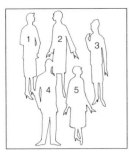

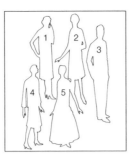

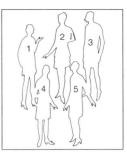

1926 Day Wear

1 Two-piece lilac wool-crêpe suit: long single-breasted collarless jacket, buttoned strap opening from high round neckline to contrasting colour hip-level belt matching cuffs of inset shirt sleeves, patterned lilac and royal blue wool-crêpe shoulder yoke matching straight below-knee-length skirt. Felt cloche hat with upturned top-stitched split brim. Leather shoes with narrow bar straps. **2** Three-piece cream wool suit: hip-length jacket worn open, self-fabric button trim above hem matching trim on split cuffs of semi-set-in sleeves and buttoned stand collar; collarless blouse with long sleeves; straight skirt to below knee, pleated front panel. Felt cloche hat trimmed with pleated ribbon. **3** Unfitted cream wool coatdress, low waistline marked with brown wool tailored belt matching front strap opening, self-fabric buttons, edge of peter-pan collar, cuffs, all edges and decorative panel seams; cream and brown patterned wool front panel, matching cuffs. Cream felt hat with wide petersham band. Two-tone leather shoes, wide bar straps, pointed toecaps, louis heels. **4** Three-piece brown and black checked wool suit: single-breasted jacket, three-button fastening, narrow lapels, flap pockets; single-breasted waistcoat with shawl collar, welt pockets; narrow trousers, no turn-ups. Coloured shirt, white collar. Yellow and red spotted silk tie. Elastic-sided leather boots. **5** Plain light grey unfitted coat, double-breasted fastening, pleated side panels from hip-level, grey and blue checked half-belt matching cuffs of narrow sleeves, wide revers, large collar and lining of wrist-length shoulder cape. Ruched velvet cloche hat, upturned brim. Black leather shoes, wide bar straps, pointed toes, louis heels.

Evening Wear

1 Coffee-coloured crêpe-de-chine sleeveless dress, low V-shaped neckline with flesh-coloured infill outlined with single row of self-fabric rouleau motifs, the same motifs in row above hemline of flared skirt on edge of brown lace side panels which match pointed side panels in unfitted bodice. Gold and brown brocade shoes. **2** Sleeveless evening dress, orange, yellow and brown patterned silk-velvet bodice, low scooped neckline, deep scalloped hemline, threaded orange velvet sash, gold satin gathered skirt and underbodice. Gold kid shoes with top-stitched detail, pointed toes, louis heels. **3** Two-piece black wool suit: edge-to-edge single-breasted jacket fastening with linked buttons, narrow inset sleeves, piped pockets, white silk handkerchief in breast pocket, silk lapels matching stripes on outside leg of narrow trousers, no turn-ups. Collarless single-breasted waistcoat. White starched shirt, wing collar. Black silk bow-tie. **4** Pale orange silk-georgette dress, wide neckline, unfitted bodice gathered above wide draped self-fabric sash edged with beads matching outsized sham buckle, flared skirt to below knee, long sleeves with circular cuffs from elbow-level, scalloped hems. Orange silk petticoat with rouleau straps. Silk shoes dyed to match dress. **5** Shiny turquoise silk-velvet ball gown, straight bodice, V-shaped insertion of flesh-coloured silk, narrow shoulder straps, ankle-length skirt gathered from hip-level over hooped underskirt, three ruched tiers decorated with jewelled straps on centre front. Gold brocade T-strap shoes, pointed toes.

Sports and Leisure Wear

1 Tennis. Collarless cream silk dress, cap sleeves, strap opening with pearl buttons, narrow revers, unfitted bodice decorated with two vertical channel seams running from shoulder to hip-level, button trim, low waistline marked with green and cream ribbon belt, pearl buckle, straight skirt to below knee, pleated side panels. Bar-strap shoes. **2** Country wear. Two-piece lovat green wool-tweed suit: hip-length double-breasted jacket, wide lapels, flap pockets, breast pocket with silk handkerchief to hip-level, box pleat. Collar-attached shirt. Tie. Trilby-style hat, high crown, narrow brim. Leather gloves. Leather brogues with tongues. **3** Golf. Lightweight ochre-yellow wool dress, unfitted bodice slightly bloused over hip-level seam, decorative front panel, button trim, pointed collar, keyhole opening, inset shirt sleeves, decorative seam above buttoned cuffs, skirt with graded box pleats, button trim. Brimless cloche hat, stitched inset bands, button trim. Lace-up leather shoes, pointed toecaps. **4** Golf. Multi-coloured knitted-wool sweater with all-over pattern, V-shaped neckline, patch pockets, inset sleeves with ribbed cuffs, matching hem. Checked wool knee-breeches. Collar-attached shirt. Tweed tie. Wool-tweed peaked cap. Knee-length knitted-wool socks. Lace-up leather brogues. **5** Bathing. Two-piece blue and white striped knitted-cotton bathing costume, hip-length sleeveless unfitted top, low scooped neckline infilled with self-fabric cross-over straps, repeated in plain fabric on front at hip-level to match hemline of top and short drawers. Rubber cap trimmed with pleated rubber flower rosette. Rubber shoes.

Underwear

1 Cream cotton combination bust flattener and corset, straight neckline, adjustable shoulder straps, stitched front firming panels, elasticated gussets from side front waist to hip-level, side hook-and-bar fastening, four adjustable suspenders. Crêpe-de-chine petticoat edged with lace. Flesh-coloured stockings. Velvet mules, satin ribbon bow trim. **2** Embroidered pale pink artificial-silk brassiere, shaped with underarm darts and gathers from central ruched panel, self-fabric frilled edging, satin ribbon shoulder straps, back fastening. Knickers in matching fabric with embroidery repeated on side hip above three tiers of frilled lace, elasticated waistband. Embroidered silk house shoes trimmed with satin. **3** Sleeveless white cotton vest, low neckline with top-stitched edge, matching armholes. Mid-thigh-length white knitted-cotton underdrawers, wide waistband, buttoned fly opening to shaped yoke seam, wide legs, machined hems. Step-in red leather house slippers. **4** Pale blue artificial-silk combination chemise and knickers, straight neckline trimmed with applied cream ribbon lace edged with satin ribbon ending in tied bow on centre front, wide knicker legs trimmed to match, decorative bib seam on front bodice, gathers on side hip, ribbon shoulder straps. Blue satin slippers trimmed with silk pom-pons. **5** Pale green artificial-silk combination chemise and knickers, hip-length unfitted bodice, trimmed on straight neckline with open embroidery and scallops of fine lace, matching hemline, wide ribbon shoulder straps, knickers gathered on hipline and into elasticated channel on hem. Flesh-coloured silk stockings. Velvet house shoes.

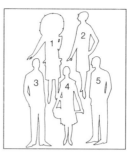

1927 Day Wear

1 Three-piece grey and brown striped suit: single-breasted jacket with two-button fastening, narrow lapels, flap pockets; collarless single-breasted waistcoat; narrow trousers, no turn-ups. White collar-attached shirt. Plain silk tie. Brown bowler hat. Leather gloves. Lace-up leather shoes. Walking stick.
2 Pink and cream checked wool dress, bound square neckline with sham keyhole opening, shirt sleeves, low waistline marked with self-fabric belt, knee-length flared skirt with shaped yoke, posy of leather flowers worn on one shoulder. Cream felt cloche hat with high crown. Leather shoes. **3** Three-piece coffee linen suit: hip-length collarless jacket, front edges and hem bound in pale blue which matches hems of inset sleeves, decorative straps, self-fabric button, stand collar and trim on blouse and hip-level inset band of knee-length flared skirt. Top-stitched straw cloche hat, high crown, wide petersham ribbon trim. Leather shoes, wide shaped bar straps, openwork detail, pointed toes.
4 Multi-coloured artificial-silk dress, boat-shaped neckline, self-fabric bound edge, inset sleeves gathered into tied cuffs, straight unfitted bodice to hipline, self-fabric sash, bow and waterfall, four-tier accordion-pleated knee-length skirt. Leather shoes, pointed toes, louis heels.
5 Navy blue silk-georgette dress, wide neckline, inset sleeves gathered into rouleau bands, unfitted bodice, panel seams with inset waterfall frills lined with bright pink silk to match overskirt effect on straight knee-length skirt, low waistline marked with narrow self-fabric buckled belt. Large fine straw hat, high crown, wide brim. Bar-strap shoes.

Evening Wear

1 Beige crêpe-de-chine dinner dress, hip-length unfitted bloused bodice, low V-shaped neckline infilled with coffee-coloured lace, embroidered collar with scalloped edge matching detail on hems of long flared inset sleeves and hem of gathered knee-length skirt. Bar-strap satin shoes. **2** Bright pink silk-georgette dress, boat-shaped neckline edged with glass beads, matching armholes, hem of hip-length bloused bodice embroidered with pearls and pink and gold beads to match scalloped hip yoke of knee-length gathered skirt, large pink silk rose worn on one shoulder. Gold kid shoes, jewelled buckles, pointed toes. **3** Black silk-crêpe dinner dress, sleeveless hip-length bloused bodice with wide neckline, straight knee-length skirt gathered into beaded jet buckle on side hip, waterfall points to mid-calf. Black satin shoes trimmed with small round buckles, pointed toes. **4** Hip-length sleeveless wrapover silver sequined bodice forming low V-shaped neckline, infilled with pink silk-satin which forms four-tier gathered skirt, three pink silk flowers worn on one shoulder, at centre of low waistline and above hem on one side of second tier of skirt. Silver kid bar-strap shoes.
5 Knee-length salmon pink georgette dress worn over petticoat with wide shoulder straps, sleeveless low scooped neckline, unfitted bodice, swathed self-fabric hip basque trimmed with spray of velvet flowers which matches spray on one shoulder, two-tier pleated skirt with uneven hemline. Gold brocade shoes with cross-over straps. **6** Knee-length green silk dress, cap sleeves, embroidered floating panel from round neckline to low hipline, matching wide hip-level belt, straight knee-level skirt with pleated side panels. Satin shoes dyed to match dress.

Sports and Leisure Wear

1 Holiday wear. Knee-length fine cotton dress, plain pink unfitted bodice to uneven hip seam, V-shaped neckline, pink and white spotted collar, matching bow trim, sewn cuffs of tight inset sleeves, side hip-belts with bow trims and flared skirt. Pink cloche hat, high crown, narrow brim. Leather shoes, bar strap with cut-out detail, pointed toes. Multi-coloured pleated-paper parasol. **2** Golf. Fine wool dress, unfitted plain grey bodice, V-shaped neckline edged with wide band of grey, blue and yellow check to match cuffs of inset sleeves and knee-length pleated skirt, low waistline marked with narrow black leather buckled belt. Grey felt cloche hat trimmed with petersham ribbon. Leather shoes with wide bar straps. **3** Single-breasted bottle green and yellow striped linen jacket, three-button fastening, patch pockets. Cream flannel trousers with turn-ups. Cream collar-attached shirt, worn open. V-neck cream knitted-wool sweater. Canvas lace-up shoes, no toecaps. **4** Tennis. Hip-length unfitted white cotton top, V-shaped neckline edged with self-fabric buttoned band and bound with contrasting colour to match bound armholes and self-fabric buttons, embroidered motif at base of neckline and on small patch pockets. Knee-length box-pleated white linen skirt with shaped yoke. Leather shoes with keyhole openings. **5** Golf. Short single-breasted brown leather jacket, narrow lapels, top-stitched brown velvet collar matching buttoned cuffs of long raglan sleeves and buttoned waistband, sloping welt pockets. Checked wool trousers with turn-ups. Collar-attached shirt. Patterned tie. Brown leather brogues.

Accessories

1 Grey felt hat, unstructured crown, wide brim turned up all round, trimmed with long red feather. **2** Cream felt cloche hat, close-fitting crown, trimmed self-fabric knot with button trim. **3** Draped silk turban, jewelled brooch trim.
4 Unstructured green felt cloche hat, brim turned up at front and back, feather trim. **5** Brimless cloche hat made from silk ribbon, silk flower trim. **6** Gold and black brocade evening shoes, gold kid straps and trim, open sides, plain black satin heels. **7** Red, orange, yellow and black striped silk turban trimmed with black velvet and jewelled brooch.
8 Felt cloche hat with close-fitting crown, draped and padded silk brim. **9** Brimless top-stitched fabric cloche hat, draped chiffon through self-fabric loop.
10 Two-tone leather shoes, buttoned double-bar straps, pointed toes, stacked heels.
11 Kid leather bag, metal frame, clasp fastening, long handle.
12 Grey felt cloche hat, high unstructured crown, wide petersham band, brim turned up at back. **13** Red velvet cloche hat, asymmetric brim turned up on one side, trimmed with bunch of feathers. **14** Short blue and white striped cotton umbrella, wooden handle, carrying strap on tip. **15** Lace-up green snakeskin shoes, pointed toes, high straight heels. **16** Small cream leather clutch bag, wraparound self-strap-and-loop fastening, top-stitched trim.
17 Short black silk rolled umbrella, curled bamboo handle. **18** Multi-coloured hand-painted silk parasol, short painted wooden handle, long carrying strap.

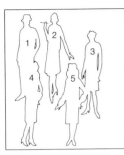
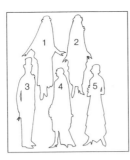
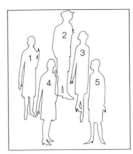
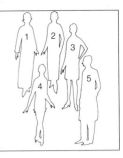

1928 Day Wear

1 Double-breasted, knee-length fitted light-brown checked wool-tweed overcoat, wide lapels, flap pockets, silk handkerchief worn in breast pocket. Wool trousers with turn-ups. Collar-attached shirt. Plain tie. Felt trilby, wide petersham band, brim turned up on one side. Leather shoes.
2 Knee-length tan-coloured crêpe dress, unfitted bodice, curved seam from natural side waist to centre-front point on low waistline matching seam from side hipline of flared skirt, vertical panel seams in front bodice, top-stitched tan-coloured satin collar matching band on bottom edge of low square neckline, hems of long inset sleeves and buckled belt. Leather shoes.
3 Knee-length fine black wool dress, asymmetric neckline bound with wide band of red satin to match waterfall and cuffs of long inset sleeves, bodice and skirt joined with knife pleats in side panel of skirt. Leather shoes, pointed toes, high heels. **4** Knee-length pale green wool coat, wrapover front, fastening with three large plastic buttons at hip-level on wide strap, shawl collar trimmed with fur to match large cuffs of narrow inset sleeves, knife pleats from side hip-level band. Brimless orange felt cloche hat trimmed with bands of cream leather. Cream leather gloves and shoes.
5 Knee-length horizontally banded red-squirrel-fur coat, wrapover front, fastening with single loop and button at hip-level, narrow sleeves with deep cuffs, large fox-fur collar. Rust-coloured felt cloche hat, wide front brim turned up, fitted crown draped with cream silk. Cream leather gloves. Brown leather shoes, small buckle trim, pointed toes.

Wedding Wear

1 Knee-length pink crêpe-de-chine sleeveless wedding dress, unfitted bodice with round neckline, flared skirt, ankle-length pink and gold lace overskirt with scalloped hem, pink velvet padded and ruched belt with large stylized self-fabric stitched bow, long free ends. Headdress of pink velvet roses, ankle-length pink silk-tulle veil. Pink satin shoes with two narrow bar straps, pointed toes. **2** Cream silk-crêpe wedding dress, low neckline edged with tiny pearls, inset sleeves flared from elbow to wrist, deep scallops edged with beads, unfitted bodice to hip-level belt embroidered with pearls and crystal beads matching floating panels of overskirt, knee-length at front to mid-calf-length at back, straight knee-length underskirt. Tiara of pearls, wax flowers and silk ribbon matching spray on shoulder, ankle-length silk-chiffon veil. Satin shoes.
3 Single-breasted dark grey frockcoat, wide lapels, self-fabric buttons. Double-breasted waistcoat with wide shawl collar. Narrow dark grey trousers, no turn-ups. White shirt worn with stiff stand collar. Striped tie. Grey top hat. White gloves. Black shoes worn with spats.
4 White crêpe wedding dress, low neckline edged with bead embroidery to match hems of tight inset sleeves, scalloped low waistline and hemline of flared knee-length skirt. Pearl bead and silk ribbon headdress, long silk veil with beaded hemline. Satin shoes. **5** Pink crêpe-de-chine bridesmaid's dress, low neckline, long inset sleeves, knee-length skirt, split three-tier pink lace overskirt, hemline dips from mid-calf-length at front to ankle-length at back, hip-level gold cord belt with tassel ends. Close-fitting pink lace cap with frilled edge, silk flower trim. Satin shoes.

Sports and Leisure Wear

1 Golf. Collarless beige knitted-wool dress, V-shaped neckline, lapels bound and edged with brown and green knitted wool which matches buttoned cuffs of tight inset sleeves, hip-level buckled belt and hemline of knee-length skirt, zig-zag seam from centre-front on natural waistline to low side hipline, double inverted side box pleats. Leather bar-strap shoes. **2** Golf. Two-piece brown tweed suit: single-breasted jacket, three-button fastening, large pleated patch pockets with buttoned flaps; knee breeches with buttoned cuffs. Collar-attached shirt. Wool tie. Brown tweed peaked cap. Hand-knitted, knee-length socks. Two-tone shoes with fringed tongues.
3 Country wear. Dark green flannel knee-length collarless coatdress, V-shaped neckline, buttoned infill, unfitted diagonally seamed bodice matching hip area of knife-pleated skirt and hems of fitted inset sleeves. Brown and beige felt hat, sectioned crown, brim turned up. Two-tone leather shoes, double bar straps, pointed toecaps, low heels. **4** Holiday wear. Knee-length sleeveless cotton dress, V-shaped neckline, plain white scalloped collar, yellow and white spotted cotton bodice trimmed from base of neckline to scalloped hip seam with white cotton self-fabric buttons, plain white cotton gathered skirt edged with scalloped band of spotted cotton. Brimless yellow and white cloche hat. Leather clutch bag. Leather shoes, buttoned bar straps.
5 Golf. Three-piece dusty-blue knitted-wool suit: collarless edge-to-edge jacket, edges bound in chocolate brown which matches cuffs of inset sleeves, patch pocket trim and buckled belt of self-fabric hip-length blouse; round neckline, self-binding, button fastening, keyhole opening; knee-length pleated skirt, chocolate brown band above hemline. Felt cloche, front brim turned up, petersham band, buckle trim. Leather bar-strap shoes.

Underwear and Negligee

1 Pale blue crêpe-de-chine ankle-length nightdress, wide ribbon shoulder straps, straight neckline edged with coffee-coloured lace which matches hem of self-fabric hip-length edge-to-edge jacket and hems of inset sleeves. Coffee-coloured lace boudoir cap, frilled edge. Velvet slippers trimmed with looped ribbon. **2** Two-piece green silk pyjama suit: hip-length unfitted top, double-breasted sham shirt front, collar and revers, shirt sleeves, double-buttoned cuffs; narrow ankle-length trousers with turn-ups. Satin house shoes. **3** Cream cotton brassiere, elasticated panel between seamed cups, elasticated side panels, back fastening. Cream cotton corset, stitched double-fabric front and side panels, elasticated panels over hips, four adjustable suspenders. Cotton waist-slip with scalloped hem. Velvet mules, feather trim, pointed toes, low heels. **4** Pale turquoise crêpe-de-chine combination chemise and knickers patterned with pink flowers, straight neckline edged with cream lace, self-fabric rouleau shoulder straps, knicker legs trimmed with double lace frill. Flesh-coloured silk stockings. Elasticated silk garters. Satin house shoes. **5** Knee-length double-breasted light blue wool dressing gown, dark blue satin roll collar piped in white to match trim on patch pockets and cuffs of inset sleeves, dark blue satin self-fabric buttons, self-fabric tie-belt. Blue and white striped silk pyjamas, shirt collar, ankle-length trousers. Step-in red leather house slippers, petersham ribbon trim.

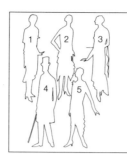

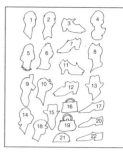

1929 Day Wear

1 Double-breasted navy-blue wool jacket, wide lapels, flap pockets. Light grey flannel straight-cut trousers, turn-ups. White cotton collar-attached shirt. Plain silk tie. White canvas shoes, pointed toecaps. **2** Two-piece wool-tweed suit: hip-level jacket with wrapover front to low-placed self-fabric buckled belt, unfitted bodice, decorative panels above hip-level pleated patch pockets with buttoned flaps, narrow lapels, fur collar matching cuffs of inset sleeves; straight skirt, inverted box pleat. Felt cloche, fitted crown, flared brim. Two-tone leather shoes, pointed toes, high heels. **3** Multi-coloured spotted cotton dress, V-shaped neckline, lace edge matching flared cuffs of inset sleeves and hems of four-tier knee-length skirt, plain cotton bow with long ends at base of neckline. Felt cloche, fitted crown, front brim turned up and edged with contrasting colour. Leather shoes, cross-over straps, pointed toes. **4** Grey wool-crêpe dress, narrow inset sleeves, sewn cuffs, knee-length skirt, pleated panel from low hip-level, short curved side panel, inset band, unfitted bloused bodice, low neckline infilled with white silk blouse-effect, V-shaped neckline, pointed collar, infill of flesh-coloured silk. Shoes with ribbon laces, pointed toes, high heels. **5** Dark red artificial-silk dress patterned with spots of light and dark blue, V-shaped neckline, narrow inset sleeves, frilled cuffs matching low curved waist seam, unfitted bodice, curved V-shaped panel seams from under arm to centre-front on natural waistline, repeated and inverted at low hip-level and above pleats on hem of straight skirt. Cloche hat, fitted crown, asymmetric split brim, self-fabric trim. Leather shoes, pointed toes, high heels.

Evening Wear

1 Sleeveless gold mesh dress embroidered all over with gold sequins, low V-shaped neckline, semi-fitted bodice to curved seam, low on side hip up to centre-front on low waistline, bias-cut floating panel from right shoulder, lined with gold tissue to match scalloped uneven hemline of flared skirt. Gold kid shoes, fine bar straps, open sides, pointed toes. **2** Sleeveless black lace dress, low scooped neckline, unfitted bloused bodice, knee-length flared skirt, wide asymmetric peach-coloured silk sash, looped low on side hip, waterfall to ankle, peach-coloured silk slip. Ostrich-feather fan. Black brocade shoes, satin trim. **3** Sleeveless cream silk-crêpe dress patterned with sprigs of embroidery, low scooped neckline, bloused bodice to low waistline, bias-cut self-fabric floating panels from each shoulder to mid-calf-length at back, straight knee-length skirt at front, curved panel seams across front hip down to side hem, gathered fishtail train from mid-calf on side to ground at back. Silk bar-strap shoes, open sides, pointed toes, high heels. **4** Knee-length fitted black wool overcoat, high front fly opening, wide satin-faced lapels, flap pockets. Black wool trousers, no turn-ups. Wing collar. White bow-tie. White silk scarf. White gloves. Black silk top hat. Black shoes. Walking stick. **5** Sleeveless midnight blue silk-velvet dress, asymmetric V-shaped neckline, hip-length bodice ruched into left side pointed inset panel from low hip-line to bustline, knee-length gathered skirt, gathered waterfall panel on left hip to mid-calf-length, feather flower on right shoulder. Cream silk shoes trimmed with gold embroidery, open sides, pointed toes, high heels.

Sports and Leisure Wear

1 Bathing. Blue and white striped knitted-cotton vest, low-cut armholes, low scooped neckline. Navy blue knitted-cotton drawers, wide waistband, button fastening, fly opening, short legs. **2** Holiday wear. Multi-coloured floral printed artificial-silk dress, V-shaped neckline, bias-cut waterfall frill from left shoulder, narrow inset sleeves, hip-length bloused bodice, diagonal panel seams, knee-length flared skirt, low curved yoke seam, low waistline marked with petersham ribbon belt. Felt cloche, fitted crown, band in contrasting colour, wide brim turned down. Matching leather clutch bag and bar-strap shoes. **3** Country wear. Light brown wool-crêpe dress, waterfall frill from base of V-shaped neckline, bloused bodice pintucked from shaped yoke seam to low waistline to match panel from elbow to above wrist in dolman sleeves, deep hip yoke, knee-length accordion-pleated skirt. Top-stitched felt hat, fitted crown, band in contrasting colour, brim turned down. Leather shoes with flat heels. **4** Bathing. Pink and blue striped knitted-cotton bathing costume, straight neckline edged with knitted braid to match shoulder straps, hemline buckled belt and panel seams. Draped rubber turban, buckle trim. Rubber shoes with bar straps. **5** Golf. Beige tweed shirt, pointed top-stitched collar, matching shoulder yoke, front button-strap opening, sleeve cuffs and single pleated patch-and-flap pocket. Brown and cream checked wool knee-breeches, waistband with self-fabric-threaded buckled belt, side hip button opening matching cuffs at knee-level, vertical piped pockets. Beige felt hat, tall crown, wide petersham band, brim turned down. Knee-high hand-knitted socks. Two-tone lace-up shoes, no toecaps, flat heels.

Accessories

1 Brimless black satin cloche, shaped band, sectioned crown. **2** Felt cloche, fitted crown, asymmetric top-stitched split brim. **3** Brown and cream two-tone leather cloche, buttoned bar straps, pointed toes, stacked heels. **4** Brimless felt cloche with earflaps, embroidered flower trim. **5** Pink felt cloche, fitted crown, self-fabric buckled band, unstructured brim turned down. **6** Brimless grey felt cloche, fitted crown, wide band wrapping over at front, fan-shaped detail. **7** Navy-blue and white leather lace-up shoes, perforated decoration, stacked heels. **8** White felt cloche, fitted crown, wide brim at front, split on one side, lined with black silk, trimmed with white ribbon bow. **9** Felt cloche, silk band, outsized bow trim. **10** Brown felt cloche, crown and brim with top-stitched detail, bow trim. **11** Leather shoes, bow trim. **12** Leather shoes, wide bar straps, openwork detail, stacked heels. **13** Light grey felt trilby, tall crown, black petersham band, wide brim. **14** Pale green felt cloche, fitted crown draped with yellow and white spotted silk scarf. **15** Grey homburg, tall crown, black petersham band matching trim on edge of brim. **16** Multi-coloured striped knitted-cotton bag, wooden frame and handle. **17** Dark brown leather brogues, perforated decoration. **18** Light brown wool-tweed peaked cap. **19** Stamped leather bag, metal frame, clasp fastening, ring handle. **20** Brown leather brogues, perforated decoration, pointed toecaps, stacked heels. **21** Sunburst patchwork leather clutch bag, metal frame, clasp fastening. **22** Dark blue leather lace-up shoes, no toecaps.

Chart of the Development of 1920s Fashion

Biographies of Designers

Sources for 1920s Fashion

Chart of the Development of 1920s Fashion

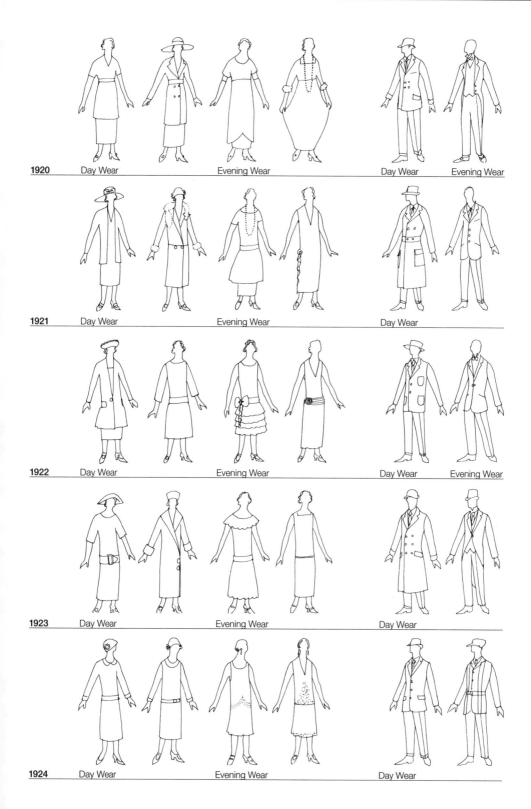

| 1920 | Day Wear | | Evening Wear | | | Day Wear | Evening Wear |

| 1921 | Day Wear | | Evening Wear | | | Day Wear | |

| 1922 | Day Wear | | Evening Wear | | | Day Wear | Evening Wear |

| 1923 | Day Wear | | Evening Wear | | | Day Wear | |

| 1924 | Day Wear | | Evening Wear | | | Day Wear | |

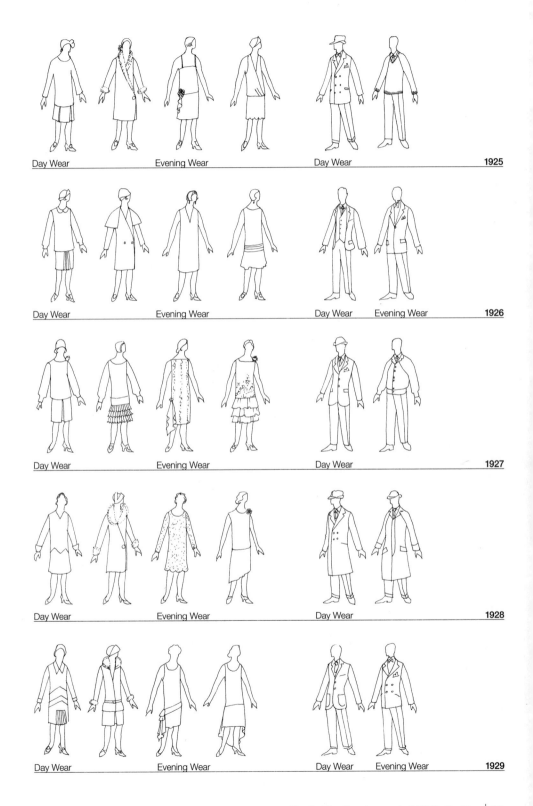

Day Wear   Evening Wear   Day Wear   1925

Day Wear   Evening Wear   Day Wear   Evening Wear   1926

Day Wear   Evening Wear   Day Wear   1927

Day Wear   Evening Wear   Day Wear   1928

Day Wear   Evening Wear   Day Wear   Evening Wear   1929

Biographies of Designers

Beer Dates unknown. Born Germany. Opened his own couture house in Paris in 1905. During the 1920s Beer was best known for elegant, conservative outfits and luxurious underwear.

Brooks Brothers Established as Brooks Clothing Company in New York in 1818, Brooks Brothers pioneered ready-to-wear clothes for men. Best known for button-down shirts, foulard ties, shetland sweaters, polo coats and for their use of madras fabric and Harris tweed.

Burberry, Thomas 1835–1926. Store owner. Born Dorking, England. After an apprenticeship with a draper, Burberry opened his own business, T. Burberry & Sons, in Basingstoke, Hampshire, in 1856. In 1891 he established a wholesale business in London specializing in waterproofed gabardine clothes for sports and leisure wear. Best known for the 'Burberry' trenchcoat which he designed for the British Royal Flying Corps during World War I and which became widely popular on the general market after the war.

Callot Soeurs (Marie Callot Gerber, Marthe Callot Bertrand, Regina Callot Chantrelle) Founded 1895. Closed 1937. Couture house. Paris. Callot Soeurs began by selling ribbons and lingerie, but became known for their elaborately decorated day dresses and heavy evening gowns. Though the house became less prominent in the late 1920s, it continued to produce high quality clothes for discerning clients wishing to avoid the harsh simplicity many other designers adopted during this period.

Carnegie, Hattie 1889–1956. Designer, manufacturer. Born Henrietta Kanengeiser in Vienna, Austria. Carnegie began her career at the age of 15 at Macy's department store in New York, dressing hats. She moved into clothing design in 1913 and launched her first collection in 1918. Her first ready-to-wear collection followed in 1928. Carnegie was best known for

grey tailored suits and black dresses which sold in her own retail stores across America. Her success was largely due to an ability to adapt Paris haute-couture fashions to the US market, where her smart but conventional clothes became highly sought after.

Chanel, Gabrielle (Coco) 1883–1971. Born in Saumur, France. Chanel began her career as a milliner in Paris in 1910, under the label 'Chanel Mode'. In 1913 she opened her first hat shop in Deauville and two years later started a dress shop in Biarritz. Her first published design, for a chemise dress, appeared in *Harper's Bazaar* in 1916. The 1920s saw her career flourish with the founding of her Paris house at 31 rue Cambon and the launch of her most famous perfume, 'No. 5'. In the same decade she was responsible for introducing the 'little black dress', wide-legged yatching pants, lightweight evening chemises and geometrically patterned beaded dresses. She also began her unconventional mixing of fabrics – plain with patterned jersey, or floral silk with tweed. In the 1930s Chanel developed the range of costume jewelry she had begun in the previous decade; her long gilt chains, rows of pearls and mixtures of semi-precious stones became particularly popular. Chanel closed her house in 1939 but reopened in 1954 with the launch of her jersey suit. She was awarded the Neiman Marcus 'Fashion Oscar' in 1955. Among the styles most associated with her name are braid-trimmed collarless cardigan-jackets, slingback, two-tone sandals and handbags with gilt chains. Her famously wearable tweed suit, which she introduced before the Second World War, is still a fashion classic today.

Chéruit, Madeleine Dates unknown. Designer. Born in France. After training with Raudnitz in Paris in the 1880s, Chéruit opened her own couture house in 1906. During the 1920s she was well known for refined,

elegant day wear and ornate evening wear. Chéruit's dresses painted with Cubist designs were also a great success in 1925. Her popularity waned towards the end of the decade and in 1935 the house was taken over by Schiaparelli.

Daché, Lilly c. 1907–? Milliner. Born Beigles, France. Following her apprenticeship with a milliner in Bordeaux, Daché worked briefly for Suzanne Talbot and then for Caroline Reboux in Paris. In 1924 she joined a small New York milliners, which she bought out almost immediately. Daché quickly became famous for her turbans, cloche hats, snoods and caps.

Delaunay, Sonia 1884–1979. Artist. Born Odessa, Russia. Studied painting in St Petersburg before moving to Paris in 1905. In 1925 Delaunay collaborated with the textile company Bianchini-Férier to produce fabric with characteristic abstract patterns in bright colours. She also worked with Jacques Heim, who made her patchwork designs into coats. Delaunay influenced many designers of the 1920s, including Patou.

Drécoll ?–1929. Couture house. Best known for luxurious tea gowns and evening dresses.

Fortuny, Mariano 1871–1949. Textile and dress designer. Born Granada, Spain. Fortuny first studied painting and drawing in Spain and then chemistry and dyeing processes in France and Germany. He invented his own textile printing and pleating processes and designed experimental, loose-fitting, exotic garments. His clients included the dancer Isadora Duncan. During the 1920s, Fortuny developed his celebrated Delphos and Peplos designs, creating sleeveless versions of his columnar dresses made from finely pleated thin silk satin. Influenced by Eastern and African garments such as the kimono, burnous and sari, Fortuny was also famous for patterned prints, gowns and veils weighted with beads, and for his use of rich silks and velvets.

Hartnell, (Sir) Norman 1901–1979. Designer. Born London, England. Worked at Madame Désirée, Esther's and with Lucile before opening his own premises in London in 1923. Hartnell's career took off during the late 1920s when he became famous for his extravagant wedding dresses, though he also designed for the theatre and for films. He was appointed dressmaker to the British Royal Family in 1938 and created Elizabeth II's wedding dress and coronation gown as well as designing many outfits for her overseas tours. His designs were central in forming the image of the royal family. In the 1940s Hartnell went on to produce his own ready-to-wear lines. During the war he designed the uniforms of the British Red Cross, the Women's Royal Army Corps and the women's division of the British police force.

Jenny 1909–1938. Couture house. Founded by Jenny Sacerdote, who trained at Paquin. Jenny's simple clothes were popular with American clients, though the house was also well known for elaborately beaded evening dresses.

Lanvin, Jeanne 1867–1946. Designer. Born Brittany, France. After an apprenticeship with Suzanne Talbot, Lanvin opened her own millinery shop in Paris in 1890. She began making clothes commercially after customers commented on the garments she made for her younger sister and daughter. Lanvin became famous for her mother/daughter outfits which were significant in the development of fashion for blurring the distinction between clothing for different age groups. Lanvin was to exert an enormous influence over the fashions of the 1920s, creating the decade's basic shape at the beginning of World War I with the chemise dress. Other designs which became characteristic of the period include her breton suits and beaded evening dresses. She was also the first couturier to design clothes for entire families, presenting her first line of menswear in 1926. The following year the first of Lanvin's famous perfumes, 'Arpège', was produced. Lanvin refused to be constricted by contemporary trends, offering an alternative to the straight silhouette of the 1920s with variations on the full-skirted 'robes de style' she first created during the 1910s. Preferring embroidery and appliquéd motifs to patterned material, she transformed motifs from orientalism, botanical etchings and Renaissance, Aztec and modern art into her own individual designs. She also became famous for her use of a particular shade of blue which became known as 'Lanvin blue'.

Lelong, Lucien 1889–1958. Designer. Born Paris, France. Lelong trained at the Hautes Etudes des Commerciales, Paris, and established his own business after the war. During the 1920s he became known for his skilful use of beautiful fabrics in creating elegant, understated dresses and eveningwear. He was one of the first designers to produce stockings and lingerie. In the late 1930s Lelong designed tight-waisted, full skirts which were precursors to Dior's 'New Look' of 1947. Lelong was president of the Chambre Syndicale de la Haute Couture from 1937 to 1947.

Madeleine et Madeleine Couture house. Founded in 1919, the house was highly influential in the early 1920s, producing varied and original garments made from luxurious materials. In 1926 it merged with Anna who, earlier that year, had created 'le smoking', a highly popular man-tailored suit.

Martial et Armand Dates unknown. A minor, though longstanding, Parisian couture house which was known more for its skill and workmanship than for innovative fashion design.

Molyneux, Edward (Captain) 1891–1974. Designer. Born London, England. Molyneux began his career producing illustrations for magazines and advertisements and in 1911 was employed as a sketcher by Lucile. After serving as a captain in World War I, he opened his own couture house in Paris in 1919, becoming famous for simple tailored suits and skirts in muted tones which were seen as archetypally English in their restrained elegance. Between 1925 and 1932 he opened further branches in Monte Carlo, Cannes, Biarritz and London. Molyneux retired in 1950. An attempted comeback in 1965 was unsuccessful – unlike Chanel, he could not adapt his understated classicism to the new times.

Paquin, Mme ?–1936. Designer. Trained at Maison Rouff until she established her own house in Paris in 1891. She was one of the first designers to open shops abroad, founding branches in London, Buenos Aires and Madrid in 1902. Though she was famous for glamorous, romantic, fairytale garments, Paquin also designed for the more active woman of her era, creating tailored suits specifically cut to ease walking. She collaborated with the celebrated fashion artists of the day, producing dresses from designs by George Barbier, Paul Iribe, Léon Bakst and Etienne Drian. The success of her exuberant, exotic styles was acknowledged in 1913 when she became the first female designer to be awarded the Légion d'Honneur. The House of Paquin remained open after her retirement in 1920, finally closing in 1956.

Patou, Jean 1880–1936. Designer. Born Normandy, France. Patou opened the small firm Maison Parry in 1912, achieving a brief success before the advent of World War I forced the firm's closure. In 1919 he reopened under his own name, producing bell-skirted, high-waisted dresses. His Cubistic sweaters were also very popular. Patou had enormous influence over 1920s fashions, in particular with his sports and bathing wear which included the calf-length pleated skirts and sleeveless cardigans worn by the tennis player Suzanne Lenglen. In 1924 he became one of the first designers to put his own initials on his clothing and in 1927 was one of the first to revert to the natural waistline. The House of Patou continued to be hugely successful after his death.

Poiret, Paul 1879–1944. Designer. Born Paris, France. Poiret worked for Doucet from 1896, moving to Worth in 1900. In 1904 he established his own house with the help of Doucet and the patronage of the actress Réjane. Poiret is widely credited with releasing women from the corseted, hourglass-shaped designs of the period, creating elegant, gently fitted dresses with fewer underclothes. He was heavily influenced by the Ballets Russes, incorporating turbans and harem pants into his collections. In 1908 and 1909 he commissioned Paul Iribe and Georges Lepape to illustrate his clothes in brochures. Poiret's 1911 design for a hobble skirt, drawn in at the ankles, caused a huge furore and brought him a certain notoriety. His house closed during World War I and though it reopened after the war and made some attempts to attract a younger clientele, Poiret found himself in the late 1920s facing financial ruin. The company finally shut its doors in 1929.

Premet Couture house. Founded by Mme Premet in Paris in 1911. Major successes of the 1920s were the 'Garconne' two-piece and the 'Gamine' oufits of 1923, which were very popular with American buyers. The house closed in the late 1920s.

Reboux, Caroline 1837–1927. Milliner. Born Paris, France. Reboux opened her own shop in 1870 and by the 1920s had become the leading Paris milliner, with a successful establishment in the rue de la Paix. During this period she created hats for most major designers and is credited with having popularized the cloche.

Redfern, John Dates unknown. Born England. During the 1850s Redfern worked as a tailor on the Isle of Wight and in the late 19th century began designing sports clothes and tailored suits for women. He reached the pinnacle of his success when he was appointed dressmaker to Queen Victoria in 1888. Though at its peak the company attracted a stylish, international clientele, by the 1920s Redfern was concentrating on simple, luxurious clothes for older women.

Vionnet, Madeleine. 1876–1975. Born Aubervilliers, France. At the age of 11 Vionnet was apprenticed to a dressmaker. Six years later she joined the House of Vincent in rue Cadot, Paris, rising to head seamstress after two years. In 1898 she travelled to London, where she worked for the dressmaker Kate O'Reilly. Returning to Paris in 1900, she spent two years as head seamstress at Callot Soeurs before moving to Doucet in 1907. In 1912 she opened her own house at 222, rue de Rivoli. This closed two years later but reopened in 1918. The late 1920s and 1930s saw Vionnet at the height of her success. Always an innovative designer, she drew inspiration from many sources, in particular Ancient Greek civilization – she was much influenced by the design of the peplos. Simplicity and austerity are at the core of her work. Vionnet was a supreme technician, draping her toiles on a wooden doll to achieve perfect proportions between body and dress. She is best remembered for her mastery of the bias cut. She retired in 1939.

Worth 1858–1954. Couture house. Founded by the English couturier Charles Frederick Worth, the House of Worth remained in family hands after his death in 1895 and in the 1920s, under his son Jean Charles Worth, it was renowned for refined, sumptuous clothes which were always at the height of fashion. The company was eventually taken over by Paquin in 1954.

Sources for 1920s Fashion

Anderson Black, J.
and Madge Garland,
A History of Fashion, 1975.

Baynes, Ken,
and Kate Baynes, eds.
*The Shoe Show: British Shoes
since 1790*, 1979.

Blum, Stella
Everyday Clothes of the Twenties,
1981.

Boucher, François
*A History of Costume in the
West*, 1965.

Bradfield, Nancy
Historical Costumes of England,
1958.
Costume in Detail, 1968.

Brooke, Iris
A History of English Costume,
1937.

Byrde, Penelope
*The Male Image: Men's Fashion
in England 1300–1970*, 1979.

Carter, Ernestine
*The Changing World of Fashion:
1900 to the Present*, 1977.

Collard, Eileen
Women's Dress in the Twenties,
1981.

Contini, Mila
Fashion, 1965.

Cunnington, C. Willet
*English Women's Clothing in the
Present Century*, 1952.

Cunnington, C. Willet
and Phillis Cunnington
The History of Underclothes, 1951.

De Courtais, Georgine
*Women's Headdress and
Hairstyles*, 1973.

Dorner, Jane
*Fashion in the Twenties and
Thirties*, 1973.

Etherington-Smith, Meredith
Patou, 1983.

Ewing, Elizabeth
*History of Twentieth Century
Fashion*, 1974.
*Dress and Undress: A History of
Women's Underwear*, 1978.
Fur in Dress, 1981.

Gallery of English Costume
Weddings, 1976.

Ginsburg, Madeleine
Wedding Dress 1740–1970,
1981.
The Hat: Trends and Traditions,
1990.

Hall-Duncan, Nancy
*The History of Fashion
Photography*, 1979.

Hamilton-Hill, Margot
and Peter Bucknell
*The Evolution of Fashion,
1066–1930*, 1967.

Hansen, Henny Harald
Costume Cavalcade, 1956.

Howell, Georgina
*In Vogue: Six Decades of
Fashion*, 1975.

Jarvis, Anthea
*Brides, Weddings and Customs,
1850–1980*, 1983.

Langley-Moore, Doris
Fashion through Fashion Plates,
1971.

Laver, James
A Concise History of Costume,
1969, revised edition 1995.
Costume, 1963.

Lee-Potter, Charlie
Sportswear in Vogue, 1984.

Lynham, Ruth, ed.
*Paris Fashion: Great Designers
and Their Creations*, 1972.

Martin, Richard
and Harold Koda
*Jocks and Nerds: Men's Style in
the Twentieth Century*, 1989.

Mulvagh, Jane
*Vogue History of 20th Century
Fashion*, 1988.

O'Hara, Georgina
The Encyclopaedia of Fashion,
1986.

Peacock, John
Fashion Sketchbook 1920–1960,
1977.
Costume 1066 to the 1990s,
1986.
*The Chronicle of Western
Costume*, 1991.
20th Century Fashion, 1993.
Men's Fashion, 1996.

Ridley, Pauline
Introduction, *Fashion Illustration
All-Colour Paperback*, 1979.

Robinson, Julian
*The Fine Art of Fashion:
An Illustrated History*, 1989.

Saint Laurent, Cecil
*The History of Ladies'
Underwear*, 1968.

Waugh, Norah
Corsets and Crinolines, 1954.
*The Cut of Women's Clothes
1600–1930*, 1968.

Wilcox, R. Turner
The Mode in Costume, 1942.
The Dictionary of Costume, 1969.

Yarwood, Doreen
*English Costume: From the
Second Century to 1967*, 1952.

Magazines
L'Art et la mode, 1925–1927.
The Bestway Bag and Scarf Book,
1924.
The Bestway Magazine,
1922–1925.
Fancy Needlework Illustrated,
1920–1928.
*The Girl's Own Paper and
Women's Magazine*, 1923–1927.
Hutchinson's Magazine,
1926–1928.
The Ladies' Field, 1920.
The Lady's World, 1920–1929.
Woman's Weekly, 1928–1929.

Dressmaker Magazines
*The Haslam System of
Dresscutting*, 1928–1929.
Weldon's Dressmaker,
1921–1925.
*Weldon's Jumpers, Blouses and
Skirts*, 1926–1927.

Women's Institute Journals
Designing and Planning Clothes,
1925.
*Designing with Foundation
Patterns*, 1920.
Drafting and Pattern Designing,
1924.
*Draping and Designing with
Scissors and Cloth*, 1924.
Dress Decoration and Ornament,
1925–1926.
Tailored Garments, 1922.
Underwear and Lingerie,
1921–1923.

Trade Journals
Costume
(Journal of the Costume Society).
The T. Eaton Catalogue
(Mail Order), 1920.
Good Style and Make,
1920–1921.

Acknowledgments

I would like to thank Liz Salmon,
Assistant Keeper of Arts, Stoke-
on-Trent City Museum and Art
Gallery, for the use of the
Museum's archives and for help
and assistance with my research.

Thanks are also due to Janet
Dunham, of Zero Antique Clothes
Shop in Newcastle-under-Lyme,
for her kindnesses and help, and
for the loan of her many costume
magazines.

Lastly, I extend my gratitude to the
Yale School of Art and Design,
Wrexham, Clwyd, for the use of
their facilities.